libra

per libris ad astra

KEVIN MILLS

INDEPENDENT INNOVATIVE INTERNATIONAL

Published by Cinnamon Press
Meirion House, Glan yr afon, Tanygrisiau
Blaenau Ffestiniog, Gwynedd, LL41 3SU
www.cinnamonpress.com
The right of Kevin Mills to be identified as author of this work has been asserted by him in accordance with the Copyright, Designs and Patent Act, 1988. Copyright © 2011 Kevin Mills
ISBN: 978-1-907090-60-8

British Library Cataloguing in Publication Data. A CIP record for this book can be obtained from the British Library.
Designed and typeset in Palatino by Cinnamon Press.
Cover from original artwork © James Ellis, used with kind permission
Printed in Poland
Cinnamon Press is represented in the UK by Inpress Ltd www.inpressbooks.co.uk and in Wales by the Welsh Books Council www.cllc.org.uk.
The publisher acknowledges the support of the Welsh Books Council.

Acknowledgements

Some of these poems have appeared in *Poetry Wales*; I am grateful to the editor. Thanks, too, to Jan Fortune at Cinnamon Press. Throughout the writing of *Libra* I have had skilled and generous readers who have helped me to hone many of these poems, especially Tiffany Atkinson, Damian Walford Davies, Lyndon Davies, Alice Entwistle, Philip Gross and Richard Marggraf Turley. Colleagues at University of Glamorgan deserve more than this mere mention for being the best I could have wished for – Jane Aaron, Gavin Edwards, Andy Smith, Diana Wallace, Jeff Wallace, Martin Willis. Thanks, as ever, for so many things, to John Schad. Others helped to make life possible through a season of pain – Andrea Hughes, Howard Hughes, Caris Jarman, Vic Mills. Special thanks to Alma and to Isla.

Biography

Kevin Mills is Reader in English Literature at the University of Glamorgan, where he teaches courses in Shakespeare, Renaissance Literature, mythology and hybrid writing. He is currently working on a critical-creative book about the Library of Nineveh. He has published a number of academic books and his first poetry collection was *Fool* (Cinnamon Press 2009).

Glossary

Adonai Hebrew for 'lord' or 'master'.
Armilla Part of an astrolabe – a component of the suspension mechanism.
Astrolabe Ancient astronomical device for solving problems relating to time and the position of the Sun and stars in the sky.
Ayia Sophia Byzantine basilica later a mosque, now a museum.
Azimuth The angle measured clockwise from the north along the horizon to the point that lies directly beneath a star.
Cresconii Wealthy Carthage family of the Byzantine period.
E.V. Rieu Editor of Penguin Classics from 1944-1964 and translator of Homer and Virgil.
Hamadryads According to Greek mythology, beings that live in, and are bonded to, trees. If the tree died, the hamdryad died with it.
Landsker Notional line separating the Welsh-speaking north from the English-speaking south of Pembrokeshire.
Limb Part of an astrolabe – the ring around the edge of the disc marked in degrees.
Manichean Of or related to the dualistic cosmology that pitted light (spirit) against darkness (material world) (3rd century CE).
Marinus Larus Marinus – Latin name for the great black-backed gull.
Mater The main part of an astrolabe – its central plate.
Ole Gunnar Solskjaer Norwegian footballer who spent most of his career at Manchester United. Nick-named 'the baby-faced assassin' due to his cherubic appearance and effectiveness as a striker.
Omonoia Greek for 'harmony' or 'concord'.
Rete A pierced disc forming part of an astrolabe.
Schrödinger (Erwin) Physicist and one of the founders of quantum mechanics.
Tympanum A plate forming part of an astrolabe.

... I suppose that even the world itself could not contain the books...
- St John 21: 25

The stars of the night
Will lend thee their light
- Robert Herrick, 'The Night-Piece, to Julia'

...various forms,
That roll'd orbicular, and turn'd to Stars
Numberless, as thou seest...
- John Milton, *Paradise Lost*, Bk. III

...leaving the tumultuous throng,
To cut across the reflex of a star
- William Wordsworth, 'Influence of Natural Objects'

... to find rhymes among the stars
- Elizabeth Barrett Browning, *Aurora Leigh*, Bk. V

Words, words. High air-castles are cunningly
built of words
- Thomas Carlyle, *Sartor Resartus*, Bk 1, Ch. 8

He thrids the labyrinth of the mind,
He reads the secret of the star...
- A. Tennyson, *In Memoriam* xcvii

I disappeared; the book grew all in all
- Robert Browning, *The Ring and the Book*, Bk. I

(here)

the   naked

                          eye

                    sees

            only

                                    in-

                    eluctable

form-
        ations   all

            else

                                    dark

(

            now)

Contents

to Ciaran Carson, for all I know

Star Manual

In the 10th century Abd al-Rahman wrote
a detailed treatise on the astrolabe

1. Abd al-Rahman

The object before me
a brass universe, 6 inches across –

everywhere
computed to the palm –

expanded in these 386 divisions I
leave to you. Should you

find
yourself telling my 1000 uses,

to the last syllable of me-
asured space,

nowhere
will be lost to you. You

will read your-
self wherever

2. Unknown

I leave
unread three hundred and eighty-six
chapters on the one thousand
uses for an astro-
labe perhaps
all the heavens might speak or do was graven on the
mater
her *limb* ringed with the ecliptic   *tympanum* and *rete*

revolving their symbols

hours
degrees

could I
read the infinite (there is

nowhere

known beyond *armilla*'s
trope) atlas

to the azimuth
of the final page-
turn   looking up
from the foot-
print of a star   I'd know
where

I leave   unread
the book that might

open
every world in these
anaphoric
lines
mark unequal hours   the
declination from
your
altitude
I

leave the
matter

10

Revelation

In 1827 Joseph Smith – founder of the Mormon Church – was visited by an angel who revealed to him the whereabouts of plates inscribed with the revelation of a new American religion

the undiscovered text
                        just
below the surface of
my backyard might be
the gos-

pel sometimes
when it rains I
think I make

out let-
ters on the dampening

slabs alpha lamb-
da just an iota
more I don't read
greek and nothing
                        true

ever spoke
english when it was
all ice

I dreamed of joseph
smith cold lenses but-

toned to the earth mutt-
erring to his angel
at the foot of the
steps
      I
         have
             no

Afterlife

When there was no
sky moonlight hardened,
wind gelled and ossified,
water stiffened
into blue bones.

Edging the tar-
mac path, fragments
of calcified breath
punch holes
in the coal-wrecked

ground, as if below
another sky had crazed,
cracked and fallen
up to our feet.
Shale, mudstone, clay,

siltstone, fine-grained, ripple-
marked, named in Latin *Argillite* –
'white clay': as
in the washed face
of a collier, the memory

of cloud, the end of
night shift. Kaolinite,
feldspar, mica, quartz
tourmaline, zircon, complex
silicates, fossil shells – access-

ory minerals bound by sweat,
spit, piss, blood, curses,
crushed limbs, organs,
hopes, black and blue
faces. This lithograph

of bruised air, suffocated
skin, glaucomaed eyes,
silted vein, frozen smoke
– a scattered source
no heaven reflects.

2

Bird Thou Wert

Corvine manichee sees mystic
meaning of shade. Hops in
circles, widdershins.
Half closed daw
winks

at right hand world, at dead
half of daylight. Pecks
at black side of
the sun.

One-white-eyed hemi-
bird purblind on
kerb-edge

picks at foodwaste -
bread, fries.

Flies.

Quote

I stop

to watch two
wrens place a potted
shrub in speech

marks. Since there is
glass, one may

be a reflection
of the other, the plant

a word be-
tween flight and light
that no-one can

pronounce.

Landsker

We called one Tosca, the other Ianto. Ancient
hardbacks of *Siarad Cymraeg* flat
on the desks. We were strangers
to Twm Sion Catti, of whom one had to
speak in Welsh. Hywel Dda and Glyndwr
buried under tons of coal, iron
and socialism.
                    Driving west from Amroth
to Newgale, rain like greaseproof over a
map. Between Tufton and Maenclochog, little
light on brown and opal edges turns fog
to floating topoi. Tosca, misty with migraine,
directed us to *tudalen deuddeg – dawelwch
bechgyn.* Ianto spat out sharp questions - *Enw?
Amser? Tywydd? Beth sy'n
bod? Beth nawr?*

Siarad Cymraeg – 'Speak Welsh' – the title of a textbook once used to
teach Welsh in secondary schools
tudalen deuddeg – page 12
dawelwch bechgyn – 'quietly boys' (imperative)
enw – 'name'
amser – 'time'
tywydd – 'weather'
beth sy'n bod? – 'what's the matter?'
beth nawr? – 'what now?'

Marinus

Looking down from Mwnt's
peak, the salt-feathered
walls of Eglwys-Y-Grog
church only gulls. The board

denies all knowledge
of the National Trust,
begs visitors for change. Inside
a framed history points to

a break of carved
beams, stairs to nowhere, absent
windows, a shadowy rev-
ivalist chapter. Across

the bay a snapped black-back
drags a wing to one last shel-
ter. The pair fumbling on
a bench do not look down.

Under Foel Drygarn

*Foel Drygarn in the Preseli hills takes its name from
the three ancient stone mounds on its peak*

What is it that teases stones
          to surface, the wind's lick
              swelling ground to hard carn-
              age? She says she's found
flint arrowheads nearby, bed-
ded in the shag of rushes,
half
          out
of the scarp's cut.
          I followed the
                  fold of its under-
                          breast,
in drizzle,   skirting
the delta of forest's
          turn,
and going

down

the rivulet's

channel. A

dowser found the stream to sup-
              ply the house – blue-
                  stone sucking
                  in essences,
gestating time. The twitch
of a wand in curved fingers
          all it takes.

18

Outcrop

Not knowing what it's called –
　　　　this place where two valleys fall
between each other's limbs –

　　　　the gaze longs for a name.
Craving the words
　　　　for a topography limned

out of silences, eyes map modal
　　　　glyphs, a body quakes
on the tongue of rock.

Fork in the Road

Sign says –   Legend says –
  St Buryan 2.   Sabbath-breakers
   Wayside stone cuts   turned to stone.
    troubled form –   Merry maidens
     Christ or Green-   sulk, lean on turf;
     man; dying   rising
      two   swallows
    arrow   for   the
    copse,   split-
    ting air.

Without

Beaupre Castle, Vale of Glamorgan: rebuilt in the 16th century by Richard Basset and his wife Catherine.

Call them Catherine and Rich-
ard, builders on ground already
layered. Say

they are storied, stone told,
one stratum
below the living, but visible

in these dressed uprights.
All eaves dropped,
trusses unjoined, tiles slipped

off, chafed walls drawing room-
ed light into
place. If they come now

unhoused,
skyroofed,
aching for what the vacant

traceries mime – a hold on
thin air – it is as if
approaching along the slow river.

Catherine (maybe)
and Richard, see the field-folded
house as a destination.

E.V. Rieu

travelled a bit with you in Argive
boats on wine-dark seas among
the dead of western islands,

the book rigged – white sail up, black
spine crewed with hulked hands.
Gods and monsters lined the gun-

wales. Home
an unravelling web of green threads. In
second-hand bookshops planets

swam into view over the Hellespont
of dog-eared, foxed and fading leaves, street
calypso musing at the door.

Sirens singing over Queen
Street, the Hayes, Morg-
an Arcade, rival a wild surmise.

Sacrifice of sun through the pane,
sharp on a Guest *Mabinogion*,
shelved. Silence of a piqued imagi-
nation.

STARSIGNS: Themis

*The Romans are said to have created the constellation of Libra
around the time they invaded Britain*

Made up

of Zuben Eschamali, Zuben
Elgenubi and Zuben Elakrab –
each a claw. Somehow the scales
obscured the clutch and venom

of the scorpion.

Romans read Libra into an
empty patch of sky. A fiction
of stars and justice for cold
nights on the western

edge.

Byzantine

for John Schad

A 6th-century Byzantine ivory panel (one half of a diptych) shows the archangel Michael bearing an orb and sceptre. It carries the inscription - 'accept these, and having learnt the cause...' The missing half may have borne an image of the emperor.

1. Antium

The right half of a poem

> accept these old men
> on sticks. Birds in trees
> the one-eyed jackdaw, hop-
> born and dying sick with
>
> cause, unhinged from
> the drowsy emperor
> left of Manichean time,
> in one another's arms,
>
> gold. Awake or
> otherwise distracted,
> dishevelled monument,
> passing, to come, or past.

2. Royal Bank of Byzantium

accept these, and having
learnt the cause of failure, try
again. You invest-
ed far too much

in the invisible, as if angels
underwrote the
loss. Here you see the simula-
crum. What you took

for real was less than
this. Half an i-
con. In the angel's hands
there is no gold. He can-

not move. A scar-
red border. An ivory ghost.
The dream of a lost em-
pire.

3. Just Outside Byzantium

Accept these, and having learnt the cause
is hopeless, you'll recall the old wreck
at the docks. A scion of Cresconii - family
motto: *loquere feliciter,* he'll tell you,
glumly. Fallen to this and a stick to boot.

Crocked, the story goes, by tackle
swinging wild in Alex. Still fingers a bi-
shop's ring, *Omonoia* cut under Christ
and the virgin. The real heresy, he dares,
is to give a shit.

                Coughs, farts, rosaries
his knuckles. Some poet, let's imagine, far out-
sold by ephemeral icons, may know – though
darkly – how to accept
it, having learnt the cause.

4. Church of Byzantium

       accept these, and having
learnt the cause
of power,
you will see it can be carved
out
      in
the domes of Ayia Sophia
and vaulted basilicas
with chiselled Proconnesian
marble, chased Sassanian silver-
ware, cut
translucent stones. Or
think of an elephant-head-
ed god – rampant among trum-
pets – hacked into angel-
ic form.

5. Sailing from Byzantium

I have accepted,
learned. It is the cause.
Scud-smothered – the sun's
breast heaving over silken traff-
ic.
A handkerchief of grass.
You putting out
lights I've left
on.
I remember a night
on the Sea of Marmara – the
moon its own icon,
my sail full of stars.
Nothing would induce
me to go

back.

6. Caveat Byzantium

accept these, and having
learnt the cause, your majesty,

take care with the hinge
that swings both ways.
Mind your fingers when you
part the wings and see

yourself pulling
back from the angel.

7. Byzantium United

accept these lessons
and having learnt the cause of your
mistake, listen again:

I said he was the archangel;
you saw Ole Gunnar Solskjaer.
Orb and sceptre, I insist,

not ball and corner flag.
I know about penal-
ties, crosses, saves,

but look at the wings.
It's true. It *was* an ivory
of two halves.

8. Schrödinger in Byzantium

Accept these. And
having learnt the cause is

quantum, trust

that somewhere
angel and emperor

meet again.

Here is the angel offering
power to

no-one.

The angel is fallen; the
emperor stands.

Neither appears.

Three Sybils

for Tiffany Atkinson

1

Sambethe was Noah's
daughter. Saw every-
thing upside-down, herself

a moon over boundless
water, a body of stars draped
with the sea. Receding, the

flood showed her a world
of rotting. Hydrophobia
worsened with each oracle.

2

I gave up counting grains
of sand when I realised
that the pain in my fingers

was arthritis. The poet
Heraclitus said – *Your soul
will revolve in the face of the*

*moon, your voice through
a thousand years.* Fuck you
Heraclitus. Fuck you.

3

It all began in Babylon. We
called it the dry Atlantis. I
left the long walls with a

bowl of fire, heading
west. Nothing went to
plan; the witch of End-

or, Circe, St Teresa. Ferry
docked at moonrise. Barking
from the quay. Where now?

Nine Books

Discovered in a warehouse in 1943, the papers of American Egyptologist
Charles Edwin Wilbour included fragmentary versions of nine ancient books.

1. Ahiqar

In the library at Nine-
veh, it is said, there was a tab-
let inscribed by Ahiqar's own
hand – a cutting of curses

not on the king who is-
sued his death war-
rant, nor on the nephew who
lied about his treachery,

nor even on the soldiers sent
to hunt him down. This:
'Cursed be the temple virgin who
exposes her face.'

2.   The Magicians

He said, Brother, I am
] a document. Keep
it secret. God
] heaven [
(bottom of column)

      Oppose
Moses who is signs
and wonders. Doing every-
thing. Then the fatal
] to mark with a chi [
(remnants of one line)

us. Make ready for
the spirit that
through a spirit
] his brother [
] weeping [
] Jambres [
(top of page)

] and a noise
(remnants of two lines)
when [his] mother
] she was amazed
(remnant of a line)
] through a spirit

(lost)

3.   More Psalms of David

151   I was the smallest killer
of a lion and a wolf.

I killed them and butch-
ered. Then I made a
flute out of bone.

He sent an angel
to listen
and learn.

I was the smallest
of all.

152   Help me. There are killers.
The dry bush leaps out.

And there is an abyss open-
ing up, Adonai,

like the mouth of
a wolf.

153   Two wild beasts, and I'm
nearly ripped. I'd be

dead if it hadn't
been for the angel. This

is his blood you see
on the wolf's teeth.

154   You need good
        people to kill
        animals and burn them.

        And you need a woman
        standing in a doorway
        singing. He likes

        it like that. But don't
        let any strangers
        in.

155   I thought he'd forgotten
        me. I was kicking
        at a dry root

        and I heard something
        breaking. It was my
        bones. I dreamed,

        ] nevertheless [

        (lost)

        (lost)

        (lost)

4.   Joseph's Dream

Verso

Recto

He now shows to the father
every cut scarred over.
He pours out grain
as twelve thin boys
look on.   He smells
the hunger of old skin-
and-bone Jacob

God of Abraham, Isaac,
(remnant of a line)
] remembering the land
of milk and honey. Famine
eats everything but the will
to live. Somewhere [
(bottom of column)

] Dinah holds out [

(traces of one lost line)

5.   The Dead Poet

As I swim I can hear – like
the filling of the king's
bath – the channels emptying
in the pool overhead.
                    Under neighbouring
walls, beneath the dry soil of the plain
where no crops grow,
it runs beyond Nineveh.
          Yesterday, king of kings,
the book of your deeds was closed,
and shelved. But this is
no desert.

6.   Orphica

Close your doors and listen. Take
the vessel – you understand me –

imagine a cloud where foot-
steps are planted, the path

of a star through the dark
sphere, the surge of spirit

in flesh at your birth, the edge
of an ocean's

edge, the shiver
of a mountain, the double image

of letters in water. Do not
betray the message. You are

its heart. Now play what you
(lost)

7.   Artapanus

Abraham taught the Egyptians
to study the stars. Deluded by
astrology, they were no match for
his descendants. Joseph invented

management, founded the Bank of
Grain. He also thought of enclosure,
double entry point scoring, and dress-
down Fridays. Moses taught Orpheus

to play the goat-
skin tabor, invented boats, animal
cults, masonry and wells. I, Art-
apanus, saw that Moses was the god

of writing. In his name I
make my book, and in the mysterious
name he could not [
(traces of one lost line)

8. Pseudo-Hecataeus

] never goes out. There is no
trace of a god. Among the heaps

of un-dressed stone are
lampstands wrought in gold –

two talents each, maybe. No
plant grows. No wine is drunk.

This is the only city in three
million *arourae.* I saw no

9. (lost)

STARSIGNS: *Antlia Pneumatica*

for Martin Willis

Nicolas-Louis de Lacaille

Boyle, perhaps. Alchemical, scientific theologian
mythologised among paradoxical stars –
crow, sextant, cup, ship and centaur. For he
breathed – we might say – ideal gas, def-
ended faith, found his law and looked for
matter transformations.
                Why not then constellate
his air pump with skylore, transmogrify stars to
such an instrument? Can we imagine it puffs at
Argo's sail to carry it south of the sea-
serpent's coils? I name also *Sculptor* and *Pictor* –
neither of much interest to the untutored eye.

Three Spirits

for the late Olaf Stapledon, author of Star Maker

1

One is on the road between
Capel Gwladys and the 'Roihi'
stone, looking at edges

of things. One is wasting fire
in black pools as the sun
sinks over Penallta. One

is dreaming of herself
falling, neither early
nor late in the day.

2

If my memory is to be
trusted: Proxima Centauri, Wolf
359, Sirius A and B, Epsilon Eridani,

Epsilon Indi, Tau Ceti, Procyon.
I've left out Barnard. You'll know
why. This is the neighbour-

hood of the sun. By
neighbourhood I mean
something like infinity.

3

One is dreaming of an-
other, rising through Hydra.
Must be April. One

is burning old diaries
in a walled garden
near the river. One

is looking up at Boötes
unsure about the myth:
ploughboy or demigod?

STARSIGNS: Sagitta

Between fox
and dolphin, winging
eagle and swan to
strike Pegasus square
on. Archer and inten-

ded victim split be-
tween traditions.
Collateral dam-
age of myth and ballistics,

a firmament of creatures
bleeds a little light
on the tele-

scoping eye.

Ghost of a Story

for Andy Smith

M. R. James, the writer of ghost stories, edited a version of the Apocalypse
of Sedrach *(c.2nd -5th century AD)*

When Christ came for him, the naïve
prophet asked where among the org-
ans of the body, his soul
rested. I will tear out, Christ replied,
your soul through your mouth, Sed-
rach. You will

feel it ripping from your finger-
nails, rooting up your heart like
the memory of death. It will stammer
from your lungs, wrench
from your follicles, bleed from your
eyes. Your knees will bend back-

wards like the devil's own and your
feet cleave like his. But
do not cry. After Christ
had harrowed Sedrach's soul,
and the paperwork was done, James
sat down to write 'Lost

Hearts'.

STARSIGNS: Vulpecula

There's no story. Helvelius

added to the sky menagerie
an arbitrary fox that fanged
a gooseneck. Yesterday

a zodiac of feathers on
the footpath, a nova
of guts and red fur on the

bypass. There's no story.

Stellophile and Astra

We are all in the gutter, but some of us are looking at the stars
— Oscar Wilde, *Lady Windermere's Fan*

She's a star, pop-
ping off to Africa for TV,
banking on her cach-
et. From a sublunary living
room, her sudden mag-
nitude is miraculous. I
enter my details. Credit
flies to the satellite

and back. She's home,
shot in a trendy bo-
rough. I'm tripping up
the High Street, lighting
out once more for Star-
bucks.

...

She's singing, spheres of light
orbiting earrings, teeth, eyes, fin-
ing skin to ether, screened
wide and flat, voiced
in Nicam. The interactive red
dwarf (please wait…), makes of her,
(loading…), momentarily,
my *Proxima Centauri*.

Cut to shanty school-
yard. Handclaps keep
time, her voice eclipsed
by a chorus, feet raising
a nebula of jumped-up
dust.

...

She drives a silver Merc convertible,
leans back on the bonnet,
fingering the three-
pronged star, a constellation
deep in the paintwork. Face
tilted to the parall-
ax of fame, she is gloss-
ed as rising.

Through the gravitational
lens and accretion disks
of copy, she flares
at dark-adapted eyes
mounted for market
penetration.

...

She's the face of a char-
itable trust formed
to save the planet and
local duck pond from devel-
opers. I went once to
feed the fowl she loves. Park-
ed - where she might
her Merc - my old Astra.

Hoped she'd come
while I tossed
bread and hummed her
hit. Rain spun rings, and
brown ducks carped
at crusts in clouded water.

...

She was on the plane, three
rows back. Reykjavik to
London. It had to be
you; I never light on seren-
dipity. Pub talk now – the close
encounter. Small auroras
in our glasses, the table a zodiac
for ring-stained heaven.

I once stood in a queue –
satellite claim – behind Olympian
Colin Jackson at Cardiff
Central, a concourse of light
in the expensive suit. Drink
up. Is that the time?

...

At this ancient church, its saint
a gob of consonants, they'll shoot
the wedding scene, locals con-
gregating – unpaid extras re-
warded by proximity. Here in person,
she'll play the bride, an open
vestibule her photographic niche.
They'll crop the slag heap, left.

Legend says the stones moved,
foundations closed, regrew
a half mile west, shoved to
sanctity and killer views by
the spirit of place. The local rag says
she has an unexpected gravity.

...

Quadrant of a room.
A stretch of dado, flowers too
fresh on the dark unit. *We knew*
when she was three or four. Always
shone at family do's, shimmying
on the coffee table, singing
to a hairbrush. Don't know where
she gets it from. Not from me,

for sure. The camera in the
lounge picks out in gibbous
relatives traces of the mass ex-
change that vamped her. Un-
sung suburb. Outer ring
road. Northern semi.

...

Ophelia Coming bombs and tabloids
pound her weight gain, circle her
thighs in the telephoto scoop. Two
months pass and its anorexia.
Hair's a nest then it's night-
club bogs. She's out of con-
trol when she slugs a papa-
razzo, verbals a stalking hack.

The chat-show incident. A kill-
ing quip on Never Mind
the Buzzcocks. Busted back-
stage at the Mercury. Mad
cow, grassed up, The Sun says
Get thee to the Priory.

...

She skins a bag of tuna
steaks, adzuki beans, a lime
and jalapeno, says she loves her
fish. What can the Michelin star
do with? Washed and julienned,
her biog spills across the
chatter, while the chef capers
with pots and puns.

A season in the TV kitch-
en takes the heat off. One
song on Woman's Hour, then
the National Lottery.
Good luck everyone. Play us
out, if you would.

...

I saved up for a tele-
scope, bought a book of charts
and myths. Last night I drew to
Lyra, the ring nebula
nothing
        but a star out of foc-
            us. Voice at the edge

        of moon-cut
                glass. Un-blue.

Wave of breath, ebbing. There's
                        Draco,
        Deneb, there

Cygnus,

            Vulpecula,

all around Vega
and
            more vague.

Hamadryads

His heart was moved... as the trees of the wood are moved

Isaiah 7:2

1

Steep
    climb to the narrow
        gate
into the wood. How   far might it be? This
time. Some woods
            migrate,   easing
limbs through stuck ground, playing with up-
        rootedness, fronds and fibres singing as
birds sing, of threat, food, shelter,
mating. Other
tunes play in and
              out,
time signatures trip-
           ping each other. He beats
a toe into leaf mould and fingers deep
        moss on the unrolled
stone, imagining the
travel   no ground, wheel, foot can
      feel . He
looks at the watch, hands trembling in the
           green
             bezel.

2

Shower-deepened
ground. He recalls at the

stone the drier
woods,

smells the spice soaking
through its changes.

Under
over-
     hangs watches traff
ic on

the flyover,
               its horizon-

tal crossed by a spi-
        ralling
            down
       into

litter – one
slow spun grace between

car   and   car.

An
ooze of moss at his

boot,   he
slips,

recovers, lets it
rain   a while,

      returns
to

Demythologising the Blackbird

A blackbird perches
on the redundant aerial.
Each time I hear him
sing I lift the sky-
light, even when it's too
cold.
This evening, a death
haunting me, the song,
full of tangled air and
light choking shelved
books. If a myth
had told this –
how he knew too late
and she was
already gone – Celts
would have made him blackbird,
pegged on the
branch of a black tree,
song leaking in through a cloven
beam, his words enough
to call her home. They would
tell you this in twighlight, smoke
and sparks, wind from the
moor, foxes barking in the
valley.
None of that – just
this attic room, hunger,
the light of a laptop, and
these few notes, pining
for woods, for dim
grass, mist, damp
leaves, for

a myth to cling to.
    I will not
        put the light on
            yet, nor go down
                into the
kitchen. The song
    ends, I close
        the roof, but
            do not go. Do not go
down.

Haunt

Castell Coch (near Cardiff) was built in the late 19th century
on the site of a 13th-century fortification

'...all in ruin no big thing, but high'
-John Leland (Tudor antiquary), of Castell Coch

Playing up to the incline
it dreams its fey
shape the revenant of

a redoubt. Look down
from a bench among the trees
and nowhere to be seen

are two who are not there. Who
do not speak of lives they do not
have, that are not built

on ruins. They do not go down
the dirt path, nor sit a while
in the car's keep. They never

will, and he will
never have driven away,
behind her, from the folly.

When he did not see her
already at the farthest
table, no hand

raised, no pen poised
over absent papers, he
could not have cast

himself in the castle's
faux knightly light –
starfucked

lover with an impotent
gaze. Coming
in from the court-

yard, he did not approach,
too little versed
in unpractised arts.

You will not know
this, but lovers do
            not build

castles

in the air.
            They rebuild
out of debris

where fall-
            en things
suggest new forms

might rise.
            This is not
for us. There are no

stones. I cannot
write
            for you. And look –

the light is lacing
courses of ashlar
            cloud.

Aseneth

...all the bees rose and flew and went away into heaven
                    — *Joseph and Aseneth* (1st Century BCE)

She cried until the ashes
at her feet turned to
mud, and then a star
entered her
room.

He said: *You are
immortal*, and he pressed
into her mouth
the wounded honey-
comb.

She saw the bees swarm
upward
as the sun grew
hot. His vapour trail
slewed west.

I spoke in
ignorance, my Lord,
but now I know. Bees
drop one by one as
if a storm

Emails from Immortals

In *The Epic of Gilgamesh*, Utnapishtim and Ziasadru are granted immortality for saving life from the great flood. But some of the gods, unhappy that humans survived, banish them to the mouth of a river. From there they have taken to emailing myself and Alma (my wife)

1

Hi Kev
Been a while. Who the hell let you into a university? Anyway – Ishtar sends her love and says can she have her Judee Sill records back. And where's my *Dorian Gray*, you thieving shit. Only joking. But I do want my *Dorian Gray* back.

Zia's OK, but gets madder by the century. Stupid cow still writes to Circe, the Witch of Endor and St Teresa. I tell her they're dead, but she doesn't listen. *You're the dead fucker*, she says, *if you don't shut up.*

Point is, Kev, can't remember what we said last time we spoke. Did I promise to send you the seeds? I think I must've. Zia says I did. Need an address though. Are you still in... wherever it was? It's good shit. PoH we called it. Species of 'Painted Death'.

Thought of you the other day cos I found my old mandolin and I was sitting in the prow playing that song you taught me – 'Somewhere, over the Rainbow'. Load of bollocks, of course. I'll tell you what's over the rainbow – me, and I'm some old, ugly mother. Not a fucking bluebird to be seen.

Have you got an email address for Robert Browning? You used to be friendly with him and Liz, didn't you? Was that you? Or am I thinking of Marggraf Turley... and Keats? Memory is shit now. Too much PoH. Who was it that burned a greenhouse full? Was that you?
Soons,
Utnapishtim
distantAssistant.com

2

Hi Alma

Sitting down with a Jasmine Tea and a crossword when I
thought of you and remembered that I hadn't told you about
Ginny. Ginny's dead, my love. Wrote that book and then died.
Still can't get over it. Drowned. So young.

Did you know we were coming back? All of us I mean. There's
this big magic hole in Switzerland made specially for us. Slow
progress but particle by particle we've got back in. Remind me
to tell you about the trip sometime. Bloody hilarious. Even
Jesus was laughing.

Thing is though, I wondered if you fancied getting together
with me and some of the girls. Remember Arachne? The one
with the legs? Taught her to weave. Well it's her and Isis,
Asherah, Danu, and a couple of the Muse girls (others are gone,
I'm afraid). They'll love you.

Only if you fancied it, I've got some Pinot Grigio and a couple
of Johnny Depps. Image of Etana that one, isn't he. If I were
4000 years younger. Still, a girl can dream. Mick and Keith are
more my league these days.

Utty sends his love. Still obsessed with boats and animals. Ugly
as ever, and d'you think I can get him to wash? Says he has a
goat for you. Dirty old sod.
Anyway, love to... thingy, and see you at night.

Ziasadru
xx

3

Kev, dude
Glad you're still alive. I had my doubts to be honest – even after
we met at Siduri's place. You looked like shit, and what were
you drinking? Pomegranate juice and Red Bull for fuck's sake.
Got your address, but can't remember why. Do you want
something?

Might sail your way soon. This estuary is a slopout, man.
Yesterday I fished out a Tesco trolley, half of a Vauxhall Nova,
69 turds, and 1961 lager cans. This morning a decomposing
piglet stuck to my rudder. I'm not kidding.

Across on the far bank I can see this thin violet beam – just a
strand of light in the middle of nothing. What the fuck is that?
The bridge is closed. Thick fog and the tide is coming in
rainbows. Immortality sucks on days like these.

Zia's playing the Rolling Stones again. I keep telling her they're
dead, but she doesn't listen. Sits there with her bottle of
Australian white, farting and sniffing and singing along with
'Satisfaction'. I swear to Enlil I'm gonna drop her false teeth in
the bay one day.

What did you want?

Utnapishtim
distantAssistant.com

4

Almsy,

Did you send those flowers? You're such a sweetheart, aren't you. How did you remember it was my birthday? I didn't remember myself until your flowers arrived. In fact, I don't think it was my birthday. I think I've used them all up.

Strange days on our boat, I can tell you. Last night I was looking up at the remnants of the stars – a few straggling wisps of anaemic light over the substation, that Nutty Utty calls a constellation. Then I thought I was having a brain haemorrhage – everything gone red.

The water was red and the sky was red and the headland was red and my body was red and Utnapishtim's face was red and the pylons were red and the tankers in the distance were red and the big birds that flew in the red sky were red.

Even the white wine was red. *Shit,* I thought, *I'm dying.* But then I remembered that I'm immortal and I knew it wasn't me doing the dying – it was everything else.

Are you OK? What colour are you? Do you like the Rolling Stones? 'Sympathy for the Devil' – that's my favourite.

Zia
xx

5

Kev
Someone came alongside in a battered old skiff this morning. Called to me. I looked over and it was a tall figure in a black cape, with a black hood. And I saw his hand and it was bones. And I looked into the hood and it was empty.

And he asked me if I still dreamed and I said: *Last night I was dreaming of a place – a valley surrounded by black mountains, and the rain wouldn't stop, and the mountains started to move and all the children were under the mountains.*

And he asked if I saw you and he said he knew you and he said he knew Alms and he said he knew where you lived and he said he loved you and he said you sang to him and he said you had no skin and he said you lived in a town where all the road signs point to the sky.

I've developed a ringing in my left ear. Zia says I should see a doctor. *The doctor's dead*, I say, but she doesn't listen. She just keeps playing the Rolling Stones and singing along to 'Paint it Black'.

I'm going to send you a parcel of eels. Cook them in vinegar.

None of this is true.

Utter
distantAssistant.com

6

Al
I'm worried about you. You looked so tired at the 60s Night.
You didn't dance at all. Not even when they played 'Let's Spend
the Night Together'. Mind you, I worry about everyone. My
mother was a worrier too. My father was half demon.

Last night Utty woke screaming. *The children! The children! The
children!* And then he ran around the boat hunting through
cupboards, pulling out drawers, turning over cushions, pulling
at the curtains and there was blood in his eyes, and he said he
must find the map.
And he found the map, and he pointed to something and he
said: *This is where the children are buried under the black mountains.*
And I looked at the clock and it said six minutes past six and it
was the morning. And his tears were blood.

I can't help him any more. I looked in the mirror and it was
empty. Did you know about my baby? I think I told you. Or
was that Rachel? I was nineteen. Why is it that immortal
parents have mortal babies?

Pray for us if you think there might be gods.

Zi
X

7

K
I need an address for you. Zia says you've moved. Moved where? Where were you?

Did you want something from me?

The water's calm but the boat feels as if it's tottering on a great wave.

What did you want?

Lv 2 A

U

8

A
Thanks for the flowers. They were lovely. And the book. I must try to start reading again when my eyes improve. It's good is it?

Not easy to see. Can't see to write much more. Everything's been red. Did I say that? Not much light left. I'll have to finish.

Thanks again.

So sweet.

Z

STARSIGNS: Scutum

for Lyndon Davies

Not of Achilles, this, but some real
        Polish king who stuck it out,

scuttled the Turks. No known
        world lives in its burn-

ish: *R Scuti*
        waxes and wanes five

months, a flock of stars they
        call the Wild Duck. Nothing

bright. You'd need an 8 inch
        telescope to know. Google *Scutum*

        and too many
                dark answers light

on white ether
        deflecting terms.

Trinity Convert

for Christine Joynes

1

I look up, apologetically,
at Newman the alumnus,
thinking about Protest-

ants and presences. Is it seven
years since I bowed out?
You'd know, perhaps, Christ-

ine. My cardinal
sin - to hang, unconverted, among
masters, doctoring the past.

2

New College Lane, sharp
about its age, undercuts the bridge,
saws through overgrowths

of stone, strips the backs of ancient
uprights, edges between
worlds. Pullman's

subtle knife - this walk
that severs skin from skin.
Universes stack up, step by step.

3

In the car, last thing, just
before the station, we recall
that there were times.

Angie, Graeme, you
and me at some pub up the river.
Oxford moves, I say,

streets swing round,
buildings creep and swivel.
You nod, indicate, turn.

Three Pools

to Damian Walford Davies

1. Bethesda

My back aches as it has
all day; you rub mosquito
bites and curse.

Boccaccio's forgiven
tomb, Fiorentino's disturbed
Christ, now this

poolside fresco.
                            Nothing but
a pump troubles the water.

                         We pick up our
loungers and move
to where we can see the moon

in olive trees. Invisible choirs
of cicadas
mass.

2. Siloam

This was the day you
pointed to Pontormo's un-
crossed lord, his cloud of
mourners looking any-

where but at him. I saw
a cumulus fantasia
of muscular colour should-
ering God offscreen. Come

evening the TV played eternal
snow and an ether
where the words *No Signal*
drifted. Defeated,

we watched Venus rise, a
cataract of moon in the pool
where the algae-eating
devil polished off blind life.

3. The Well

I think it was Castellina, he lay
staring down into a portal.

All we saw was Tuscan sun glancing
back – no depth possible. The boy

ran off, calling to an unseen
father. The church locked again,

our hunt for relics dead,
we looked for a beer.

Longshore Drift

If this window, opening   over
                              roofs,

enclosed the sea,

heard not traffic but
diastolic drawing

of the tide, penned
two faces

rather than
one,

this would
be an atlantic   reach,
        inland,

the heart's breakers
a rhythm written

into
littoral geo-
graphy.

One
or two

mornings,
shod

with patent moons,
leaving no print   in the sea-
grit,

one
or two

                  walkers
           find the angle
    of approach

    that fetches the
    strand
    to their
    foot-
        fall.

Feste and Him

No pains
sir I take pleas-
ure in singing sir
it raineth every
day I live
by the church take away
the lady I am indeed
not her fool but her corrupter
of words words are very
rascals I do but read mad-
ness misprision in the high-
est degree I am one
of those gentle ones
that will use the devil
himself with courtesy to please
you every day sayest thou
that the house is dark I am
gone sir nothing that is
so is so I
will fetch you light
and paper and
ink

6

Dehiscence

The Royal Library of Ashurbanipal at Nineveh, containing thousands of clay tablets, was discovered by the 19th-century archaeologist Austen Henry Layard.

When Lay-
     ard broke

      ground, all the books
of Nineveh flowered from
clay. Ancient
Gilgamesh greened into modern
light,   worlds
grew into thickening

time.

     Tiny deltoid forms of
cunei opened

       from their
roots in red-brown fields, winged
bulls narrowed pass-
ages, servants bore fruit, fourteen
horses
     bowed to the man-
fish. A long

exordium in stone

reft

     between kings
and twelve great gods,
Astarte parted
from

/saːmz/

To the tune of 'Do not Destroy' (Psalm 75)

1. Wicked foreigners are jackals
and the king is a powerless supplicant.
2. Strangers are dogs
but the king is a pussycat.
3. Remember the quails and manna?
Good wasn't it. Those were the days.
Tables are likely to be laid
4. in improbable places.
5. Food yesterday and water tomorrow
in the valley of the shadow.
Don't worry.
6. Storms make me think of God.
People are sheep.
7. Singing to the Lord is marvellous.
Now say it with me:
singing is marvellous in his ears.
Se'lah

8. I am lonely and no-one understands me
because I love God and they love horses.
9. My enemies are stupid. God is clever,
and he's bigger than their gods.
10. God feeds wild animals and keeps
the weather in a lock-up.
11. I know three things;
four things I've been told:
a horse is not as good as God;
12. He casts his shoe at Ephraim;
there were quails and manna;
13. God is better than many horses.
14. Women are OK for a laugh,
but men are lovely.
15. I am a warrior. Look at these arms.
16. I am a bowman without equal;

17. I can shoot the hyrax at forty paces,
the coney at fifty.
The rock badger is not safe
even at a hundred paces.
18. You can't hide from God.
Not even when you're dead.
No, not even when you've been dead
for quite a while.
9. Everything belongs to God,
and nothing belongs to you.
Some stuff is mine though,
because God gave it to me.
20. Moab is my washpot.
21. He likes me because I say
what he wants to hear.
22. Praise the Lord.
23. God's laws are fascinating;
I read them all the time,
and I can say them off by heart.
24. Life is shit most of the time,
but praise the Lord,
25. or he'll make it worse.

Se'lah.

Jeremiad

When thou hast made an end of reading this book, thou shalt bind a stone to it, and cast it into the midst of Euphrates

(Jeremiah 51:63)

written
  words can't
    breathe. They drown. Even
     those that float a while

      soak up time,

      resist the blurring sur-
    ge, flood of verbs, only to di-
sin-
teg-

  rat-
e, from book
to cedilla,
   in the speaking

  tsunami. Euphrates –

   from old
    Persian *Ufratū*, and this
     from *Purat*
  or *Puratu* – the river.

   Sometimes *Pura-
nun* – the great
river.

  Flowed through
Gen-
   esis (ch. 2 v.